A HISTORY OF THE FRENCH LEGATION IN TEXAS

Alphonse Dubois de Saligny and His House

KENNETH HAFERTEPE

TEXAS STATE
HISTORICAL ASSOCIATION

Library of Congress Cataloging-in-Publication Data

Hafertepe, Kenneth, 1955–
    A history of the French legation in Texas.
    (Popular history series ; no. 4)
    1. French Legation (Austin, Tex.) 2. Dubois, de Saligny A.—
Homes and haunts—Texas—Austin. 3. Austin (Tex.)—Buildings,
structures, etc. 4. Texas—History—Republic, 1836–1846.
    I. Title. II. Series
F394.A98H34 1989   976.4'31   89-4604
ISBN 0-87611-087-1

Cover: The French Legation (detail) by Julia Robertson, c. 1858.
Oil on canvas, 15 ¹/₄ × 19 ¹/₄ in. *Courtesy French Legation Committee,
Daughters of the Republic of Texas.*

CONTENTS

To Mrs. Joe L. (Lois) Douglas
Chair, French Legation Committee
Daughters of the Republic of Texas
and
John J. Cleary
Director, French Legation Museum
Friends through thick and thin

ACKNOWLEDGMENTS

THIS PROJECT WAS RESEARCHED AND WRITTEN under the administration of Mrs. Joe L. (Lois) Douglas, chairwoman of the French Legation Committee of the Daughters of the Republic of Texas. Lois has been a determined supporter of this book since its inception and has discussed it with me word-for-word. I deeply appreciate her caring and her commitment to historical accuracy. Other members of the DRT have also been supportive of this effort. These include Mrs. Grady D. (Martha) Rash, Jr., president-general of the DRT, 1985–87, Mrs. David L. (Karen) Thompson, Mrs. Sam G. (Belle) Cook, and Mrs. Jerry A. (Lel) Hawkins. The director of the French Legation Museum, John J. Cleary, has patiently listened to my many ruminations, provided valuable criticism, and been a stout defender of historical verity.

In researching this book I have mined a number of archives. Three have been especially useful: the Austin History Center of the Austin Public Library, the Barker Texas History Center at the University of Texas at Austin, and the Texas State Archives. In particular, Michael Green of the State Archives was persistent in tracking down obscure items for me. The Texas Archeological Laboratory at the University of Texas opened to me its files on the 1966 dig on the site of the original kitchen. At the Archives of the Catholic Diocese of Austin, my research was aided by Kennon Garafalo and later by Gary Bryson. Dorothy Kaiser of Kenrick Seminary, Saint Louis, Missouri, Gerry Hartel and Judy Kirn of the Library and Archives, St. Mary's Seminary, Perryville, Missouri, and Sharon Sumpter of the Archives of the University of Notre Dame were prompt and helpful in my research by mail.

I have benefited from the critical expertise of a number of individuals. These include John Ferguson, formerly of the Texas Historical Commission; Michael McCullar, architecture critic for the Austin *American-Statesman*; C. C. Pinkney, landscape architect; and David Rifkin of the Texas Parks and Wildlife Department. Mrs. Joan Clay Lowe's thorough evaluation of the furniture and other artifacts informed my discussion of these objects. The manuscript was read by Dr. Nancy Nichols Barker of the Department of History, University of Texas at Austin, whose two-volume work on *The French Legation in Texas* is a distinguished piece of scholarship, and by Professor Eugene George of the Department of Civil Engineering, University of Texas at Austin. Their comments were highly stimulating and improved the manuscript a great deal.

At the Texas State Historical Association, Dr. George B. Ward first suggested that the TSHA might be interested in publishing the book, and Dr. Ron Tyler, the director of the TSHA, also lent his support.

As always, my parents, Charles and Gloria Hafertepe, have weighed in with financial and moral support. And my wife, Kim Troutman Hafertepe, has cheered with me during the ups and consoled me during the downs. She is unflagging in encouragement and in love. As in all I do, a bit of her is in this book.

INTRODUCTION

PERCHED ATOP ITS HILL just east of Interstate Highway 35, the old French Legation looks out on downtown Austin, Texas. The changes that this old house has survived have been momentous. When the French Legation was built in 1840 and 1841, Austin was little more than a year old and consisted mainly of log buildings. The only two-story structures were the President's House and a hotel, Bullock's Inn. From the front porch of the Legation one could watch the construction of the 1850s Greek Revival Capitol and, when that building burned, of the great Renaissance Revival Capitol that stands today, its dome still visible from the porch of the Legation. In this century progress has eradicated all other evidence of the Austin that the builders of this house knew, save the street plan. Where Bullock's Inn once stood on the northwest corner of Sixth and Congress, a giant office building now sprawls. The site of the wood-frame President's House is now occupied by a granite and steel hotel and office building. And the site of the temporary Capitol of 1839 is marked by an inconspicuous plaque on Austin's equally inconspicuous Municipal Building. The French Legation stands as a lone remnant of Austin's earliest days—the days when Texas was a young republic, receiving in its new capital diplomatic representatives from the more polished cultural climes of Paris, London, and Washington. This little book is about one of those diplomats and about the pioneers and politicians with whom he lived. It is also about one pioneering Austin family, who bought the French Legation and made it their home. And it is about the many women and men who have recognized the historic importance of this old building and have given of themselves to preserve it.

1.
THE FRENCH LEGATION IN TEXAS

I N FEBRUARY, 1839, Jean Pierre Isidore Alphonse Dubois de Saligny, a representative of King Louis Philippe of France, arrived in the dusty little town of Houston, the capital of the Republic of Texas. Dubois was a secretary—that is, an administrative assistant—at the French Legation in Washington, D.C. His superiors sent him to investigate whether the French government should officially recognize Texas as an independent nation-state. He spent a month or so in Texas, meeting with government officials and writing reports to the foreign minister in Paris. In a manner that foreshadowed his later difficulties with the Texians and with his own government, Dubois was less than truthful in his reports. He claimed to have visited Nacogdoches and San Antonio—in what must have been record time—and neglected to mention that he had taken a vacation to New Orleans. He did, however, write a stirring conclusion in his report to the foreign minister: "The recognition of the independence of Texas by the Government of the King will bring great advantages to France for many years to come. We have a glorious opportunity before us; we must not let it escape us." The government was persuaded—on September 25, 1839, France recognized the Republic of Texas by signing a Treaty of Amity, Navigation, and Commerce.[1]

Dubois was an ambitious young man seeking to further himself in the French foreign service. He was the son of Jean Baptiste Isidore Dubois, a tax collector, and Marie Louise Rose Bertrand.

Jean Pierre Isidore Dubois de Saligny, by unknown artist, c. 1841.
Location of original unknown. *Courtesy Barker Texas History Center,
The University of Texas at Austin.* An ambitious young diplomat,
Alphonse Dubois, the supposed Count de Saligny, made quite an
impression in Texas, but not the type of impression he intended.

The Dubois family seems to have moved from Normandy to Paris
sometime after the birth of Alphonse in 1809. Luckily for young
Dubois, he became a schoolmate of King Louis Philippe's eldest
son, Prince Ferdinand, who helped him to enter the diplomatic
corps. Having served as secretary at legations in Hanover (Ger-
many), Greece, and the United States, Dubois was promoted to
charge d'affaires and assigned to establish a legation in Texas.[2]

Today all nations send ambassadors to each other and set up
embassies, but in the nineteenth century only the great powers
sent and received ambassadors. In dealing with lesser states a
great power like France would send and receive a minister, who

would operate a legation. Fledgling states—like Texas—were entitled to a legation, but without a minister. Instead, an officer of lower rank was left in charge—a chargé d'affaires.

Thus, on his appointment as chargé d'affaires, Alphonse Dubois moved up a rung on the ladder of diplomatic advancement, but he was still a very junior official. He was certainly aware of this; and, perhaps to lend himself needed dignity, on arriving in Texas he declared himself a count and added "de Saligny" to his last name. Some Texans called him Count de Saligny, others called him Mister de Saligny. The French foreign minister humored Dubois de Saligny about his newly expanded last name, but crossed out the title "count" whenever he found it in reference to Dubois.[3]

When Dubois de Saligny arrived in Austin at the start of February, 1840, the town was less than a year old. Mirabeau B. Lamar, president of the Republic of Texas, had personally chosen the site of Austin in 1839; in May of that year, he sent Edwin Waller and a crew of carpenters and other workmen to construct a capital city. By October, they had built a temporary Capitol, a President's House, and a great many log houses, some of which served not only as residences but also as offices for the secretaries of state, war, and the treasury. At the northwest corner of Congress Avenue and Pecan (now Sixth) Street was Bullock's Inn, a two-story house with several adjacent log cabins, run by Richard Bullock. In 1840, Austin was a tiny town on Texas's western frontier, and its 856 inhabitants lived with the constant threat of Indian attack.[4]

Into these primitive, frontier conditions rode a diplomat used to cosmopolitan Paris. He did attempt to bring with him the comforts of home: he was accompanied by a secretary, Jules Dulong, who was to assist with the business of the legation, and two servants, Eugene Pluyette, his butler, and Charles Baudin, his Parisian-trained cook.[5] His reception in Austin, Dubois reported, was very friendly. Edwin Waller, the first mayor of Austin, and several other leading citizens met him outside the town and escorted him to the lodging they had reserved for him. But Dubois seems to have stayed only long enough to exchange the Texan and

City of Austin the New Capital of Texas in January 1, 1840. Edward Hall, in *A History of Texas, or the Emigrant's Guide to the New Republic,* 1844. Lithograph. 4 x 7 ³/₁₆ in. *Courtesy Barker Texas History Center.* This 1840 view depicts Austin in its infancy: Congress Avenue led up to the future site of the State Capitol, and Pecan Street was the only east-west thoroughfare. On the hill east of congress was the President's House, to the west of Congress was the temporary Capitol, and on the northwest corner of Pecan and Congress was Bullock's Inn.

French ratifications of the treaty by which France and Texas recognized each other. Then he left for another trip to New Orleans.[6]

When he returned to Austin in late July, 1840, things began to go very wrong. Dubois found the little town "almost deserted": more than two-thirds of the inhabitants—some six hundred people—had left at the close of the last session of Congress.[7] His journey back had been slowed by "the terrible, burning heat of the sun in this country."[8] While in New Orleans Dubois had bought three slaves, Henry, Rosanna, and Flora, to take the worst work off the hands of his French servants Pluyette and Baudin. Flora, however, died shortly after she arrived in Austin, from an illness "caused by the hardships of the journey."[9]

A day or so after his arrival, a controversy arose between Dubois and James Latham, the teamster who had carted his furniture and goods all the way from the coast. Latham's fee was $300; Dubois paid in six $50 bills, which Latham immediately suspected were counterfeit. His suspicions heightened when Dubois refused to take them back or to give him other bills. Latham filed a complaint with the secretary of the treasury, James Harper Starr. When Starr saw the bills, he knew at once they were fake and gave Latham real Republic of Texas money. Starr and his fellow cabinet officers took the loss upon themselves, rather than get off on the wrong foot with the French representative. Dubois himself may have been fooled into accepting these phony bills in New Orleans, but it is unfortunate that he tried to pass them off on a teamster.[10]

For a few days, Dubois stayed at Bullock's Inn while he waited to occupy the house he had agreed to rent on the southeast corner of Pecan (Sixth) and Guadalupe, three blocks from Bullock's Inn on the western edge of town. It was quite small and made of pine boards; indeed, Dubois referred to it as "a wretched wood shanty of three rooms, for which I pay the *trifling sum* of 100 dollars per month!" He was renting this house from Captain Jesse Billingsley, a veteran of the Battle of San Jacinto, who resided on his farm in Bastrop County. Most early residents of Austin lived either at Bullock's or in log cabins, but Dubois was willing to pay a premium for his own house, even for his own shanty. He was aware that it would take months to acquire land and to build a house and wished to begin immediately the process of wining and dining the prominent members of the Texan government. It was in this house that Dubois lived during most of his stay in Austin.[11]

In the month of December, 1840, Dubois entertained house guests as well. Jean Marie Odin was a French priest and vice-prefect apostolic for Texas whom Dubois had met in New Orleans. Odin stayed with Dubois the entire month of December and was joined for part of it by his superior, Father John Timon, an American priest born of Irish parents. Odin and Timon hoped to convince the Texas Congress to return to the Catholic Church the missions seized during the Texas Revolution. Dubois promised to wield all his influence to help them. Odin recorded in his diary "a great dinner" at Dubois de Saligny's, attended by Sam Houston and many members of Congress. This was the first of several such dinners given by Dubois. Much to the joy of Fathers Timon and Odin, the Texas Congress voted to return all the missions to the Church—even the Alamo.[12] No wonder Odin considered his meeting Dubois providential!

Richard Bullock, however, did not consider *his* meeting with Dubois to be a gift from God. In fact, he claimed that Dubois still owed him for board from July. His complaints were so vociferous and so abusive that Dubois turned to the Texas government, convincing it to pass a law to punish by fine and imprisonment "any individual who should speak in disrespectful terms of any Foreign Minister accredited to the Government."[13] Alas, even this could not curb Bullock's tongue.

Meanwhile, Dubois was trying his best to improve the social life of the tiny frontier capital. He write to the foreign minister that "twice a week during the session I intend to invite some of the most influential men of the country to my house either for dinner or the evening."[14] (His house was the rented one on Pecan Street; at that time, the Legation was barely begun.) Dubois's dinners were elaborate affairs, at which the butler Eugene Pluyette served the culinary masterworks of the Parisian-trained chef Baudin and the wines that Dubois had brought from France. Baudin's specialties were cakes, candies, and other confections; when Dubois left Austin for New Orleans, his chef stayed behind and opened a confectionery on Congress Avenue, where, an advertisement claimed, "the public will always find a large assortment of Cakes of the best quality, Bonbons, and every variety of Candies."[15]

One Texan who found himself dazzled by Dubois's dinners was Isaac Van Zandt, the congressman from Marshall. In December, 1840, he wrote to his wife describing a dinner attended by Sam Houston, Father Odin, and several members of the Texas Congress: "It was the most brilliant affair I ever saw, the most massive plate of silver and gold, the finest glass, and everything exceeded anything I ever saw. We sat at the table four hours—I was wearied to death but had to stand it with the company. We had plates changed about fifteen times."[16] If Van Zandt was wearied, the servants Pluyette and Baudin must have been exhausted!

What Dubois was seeking to promote at these lavish dinners was the Franco-Texian bill, which Congressman James Mayfield introduced in the House of Representatives in January of 1841. This bill would create a corporation to explore and settle the wilds of West Texas. This corporation was to hire geologists, mineralogists, and botanists to assess the natural resources of the region, and to recruit at least 8,000 French colonists within an eight-year period. In return the corporation would receive the patents to three million acres of land, a tax exemption on that land until 1845, the right to duty-free importation of European goods, and the right to extract minerals and precious materials, with fifteen percent of the profits going to the Texas government. Although such leading Texans as Sam Houston and Anson Jones favored the bill, there was intense opposition as well. James Mayfield, who had introduced the bill, had a falling out with Dubois and became a fierce opponent of the measure. It became a point of controversy in the presidential election of 1841 and was never passed.[17]

Dubois—and many Texans—thought that Austin would have easy access to Santa Fe and hoped to tap that town's rich trade.

View of Pecan Street Looking east from Congress Avenue, c. 1841. Engraving after a drawing by Julia Robertson. From the Galveston *Daily News,* February 16, 1896. *Courtesy Rosenberg Library, Galveston.* This view of East Pecan Street shows the one-story building (number 5) which served as the store of Jules Dulong and as the office of the French Legation. It was through the door of this building that Eugene Pluyette dove to escape the wrath of Richard Bullock for having killed several of the innkeeper's pigs.

Jules Dulong, who had come to Texas to serve as secretary at the French Legation, resigned his position and opened a store on Pecan Street, in the same building that housed the office of the Legation. While awaiting the arrival of treasures from Santa Fe, the principal items in the store were fine wines, champagne, and French cordials. Dulong's hopes must have died with the Franco-Texian bill, because his mercantile establishment was never heard from again.[18]

But the low point of Dubois de Saligny's stay in Austin was the Pig War. The innkeeper Richard Bullock owned a number of hogs, which he let have the freedom of the town. These porkers were an aggressive sort and would trot down Pecan Street three blocks to Dubois's "wretched wood shanty."[19] There they would work away at the fence to get into his courtyard. "Every morning," the chargé wrote, "one of my servants has to spend two hours in repairing and nailing up the rails of the fence that these animals trample down to get at the corn for my horses." As time

8

went on, the pigs grew more brazen. "One day three pigs even penetrated to my bedroom and ate my linen and destroyed my papers."[20]

Finally, Dubois ordered his servant Pluyette to kill any pigs that came into the courtyard. We shall never know for certain how many pigs perished at Pluyette's hand. Bullock claimed that between fifteen and twenty-five hogs "have been most maliciously and wantonly killed with pitchforks and pistols."[21] Dubois conceded that five or six pigs had been killed, but argued that they had received their just desserts. Twice when Pluyette and Bullock met on the street they scuffled, but on the morning of February 19, 1841, war broke out. Moses Johnson testified that he saw Bullock running after Pluyette, throwing rocks at him and threatening him with an axe. Pluyette put down the basket he was carrying and fought with Bullock for some two minutes, each man kicking and punching the other. When Bullock hit the Frenchman on the head, blood streamed down his face, and he ran toward the store of Jules Dulong, with Bullock in hot pursuit, wielding a club. Nearly blinded with blood, Pluyette dived into Dulong's door. Dulong testified that Bullock did not come in, but stood outside using abusive language.[22]

Bullock's actions infuriated Dubois, or so he claimed. In a letter to James Mayfield, who was then secretary of state, Dubois wrote that these acts "constitute one of the most scandalous and outrageous violations of the Laws of Nations." In the view of the chargé, Pluyette as a French national was entitled to the protection of the host government.[23] Mayfield regretted Bullock's actions, but insisted that the proper avenue for punishment was through the local courts. Bullock was arraigned on February 22; amazingly, Dubois refused to allow Pluyette to testify, again citing "the Laws of Nations."[24] As if this were not enough, the next session of district court was not until November, and John Chalmers, the secretary of the treasury and a relative of Mrs. Bullock, appeared to stand as bail for the innkeeper.[25]

Dubois began a heated correspondence with Secretary of State Mayfield. The charge could not believe that "a cheat and a bully" like Bullock could get away with assault and battery on a foreign national.[26] Worse was to come. On the evening of March 24, Dubois attempted to pay a visit to the chargé d'affaires of the United States, Colonel George H. Flood. Unfortunately, Flood lived at Bullock's Inn; when Dubois tried to enter, the innkeeper forbade him the door. An argument ensued, and Bullock announced that "the next time you come here I will beat you to death. Now I have warned you; in the future I shall act, not talk." The two men argued further, then Bullock grabbed Dubois and shook him, first by the collar, then by the arm. The diplomat boasted to Mayfield that his composure disconcerted Bullock and that he was able to walk on his way as Bullock hurled further insults behind him.[27]

Dubois may have kept his composure in this confrontation with Bullock, but not when he heard the reaction of John Chalmers, the treasury secretary. Chalmers not only voiced approval of Bullock's actions, but said that if he had faced Dubois he would have pulled out his gun and killed him. Needless to say, Dubois was somewhat miffed by this. He demanded "immediate and energetic measures" to punish the "outrages" of Bullock. Secretary of State Mayfield, however, was not sympathetic to the demands that Bullock be punished without due process. Indeed, he was beginning to think of Dubois as "that insolent foreigner." On April 8, Mayfield wrote to George McIntosh, the Texas chargé in Paris, ordering him to ask for the recall of Dubois de Saligny. Mayfield's letter accused Dubois of paying his teamster with counterfeit money and of standing to profit enormously from the Franco-Texian bill. Dubois, meanwhile, grew impatient of waiting for Bullock's punishment; on April 29, 1841, he set off for Galveston, never to return to Austin.[28]

By May, word of the Pig War was spreading across Texas. Indeed, the pigs were becoming something of a *cause célèbre*. The San Augustine *Journal and Advertizer* of May 20, 1841, editorialized about the "haughty temper" of Dubois de Saligny and warned against becoming too entangled with France. The editorial concluded with the stirring battle cry: "Go it Texas! Viva la pigs!"[29]

Dubois left Galveston for New Orleans on May 15 and stayed

there for some ten months. From New Orleans he observed the heated presidential election of 1841 between Sam Houston and David G. Burnet, who had been acting president during the long illness of Mirabeau B. Lamar. Houston's victory meant the removal of Dubois's worst enemies, Mayfield and Chalmers. At the State Department Mayfield was replaced by Dubois's friend Anson Jones. Moreover, Dubois was delighted when Houston and Jones recalled George McIntosh, the Texas charge in Paris. His replacement was Dr. Ashbel Smith, whom Dubois considered "an intelligent man" with "a high regard for France."When Smith stopped in New Orleans on the way to Paris, he asked Dubois to return to Texas, which the French chargé finally did in April, 1842. At that time President Houston was attempting to move the capital to Houston or Washington-on-the-Brazos; Dubois shuttled between Galveston and Houston, never getting as far as Austin. This stay in Texas was quite brief: in October, he was back in Paris on a leave of absence, ostensibly for reasons of health.[30]

During his absence the French government sent an interim chargé d'affaires, Jules Edouard Fontaine, Viscount de Cramayel, but Dubois returned to Louisiana again in January of 1844. He claimed to be travelling back and forth from New Orleans to Galveston, causing the French foreign minister, Francois Pierre Guillaume Guizot, to write on the margin of one of Dubois's reports, "Why all these continuous comings and goings? The rule is that an agent must not leave the country to which he is accredited without authorization. Remind M. de Saligny of this." Dubois's restlessness continued until his recall, which came after the Republic of Texas joined the United States in February of 1846.[31]

The mission of Dubois de Saligny to Texas was an unmitigated failure, and the French Foreign Ministry knew it. Ashbel Smith, the Texas chargé in Paris, recalled having been told that Dubois was "in bad odor at the Foreign Office" over the Pig War. Admiral Charles Baudin (no relation to Dubois's chef) told Smith that "France might afford to do wrong, [but] she could not afford to be rendered ridiculous." When Dubois returned to Paris, he was pointedly refused an audience with the foreign minister in which

11

he might explain his conduct. His service to the government of King Louis Philippe was over.[32]

New possibilities arose with the overthrow of Louis Philippe in 1848. The new government of Louis Napoleon Bonaparte promoted Dubois to the rank of minister and assigned him to direct the French Legation at the Hague. Dubois seems to have been no more popular in the Netherlands than in Texas; after two years, he was abruptly recalled. He then languished in diplomatic limbo until 1860, when he received an appointment as French minister to Mexico. In this position Dubois did much harm, encouraging Emperor Napoleon III to send troops into Mexico to support the Mexican monarchy of Maximilian and Charlotte. This had tragic consequences for both France and Mexico, embroiling the French in a military operation to prop up a monarchy that had no popular support. Only Dubois profited from the situation: just before he was recalled, he married a young Mexican woman from a wealthy and ultraconservative Catholic family.[33]

Dubois took her back to France and with her money bought a chateau and a large estate in Normandy, the region of his birth. Here he lived for the last twenty-five years of his life. Even in Normandy Dubois was no more popular than in Texas or Mexico. Rumors abounded of his cruelty toward his wife and his servants. But after his death in 1888, the locals got even. When the cemetery was moved from the town square to the area behind the church, the townspeople refused to move Dubois and simply removed his tombstone. Thus, when festivals are held in the square, the locals dance on his grave.[34]

2.
THE MANSION OF
THE LEGATION

DUBOIS DE SALIGNY was never very happy about his accommodations in Austin, his "wretched wood shanty of three rooms." On November 6, 1840, he complained to the French foreign minister: "I have been unable to find a suitable lodging," noting that he had resigned himself "to receiving guests in this humble dwelling where I am now camping, rather than living, and I do the honors of the house as best I can."[35]

He therefore decided to build his own house. Toward that end he purchased, on September 15, 1840, "a beautiful piece of property" from Anson Jones, whom he had known in Washington, D.C., when Jones had been Texas chargé to the United States. The land Dubois bought from Jones was a little more than twenty-one acres just beyond the original boundary of town. It stretched from East Avenue (the present-day Interstate 35) to what is now San Marcos Street, and from Seventh Street north to Eleventh Street.[36]

In the letter to the foreign minister quoted above, Dubois mentioned that he was having "difficulty in obtaining building materials" for his house and that he was further delayed by the illness that kept him bedridden throughout most of August, September, and October. Indeed, he feared that he would not be able to move into the house before the spring. It is most likely, therefore, that work did not begin on the house until December of 1840 and that it was not completed until the middle of 1841.[37]

Almost before work was begun, Dubois sold the house and land to his friend Father Jean Marie Odin. In a deed dated December 29, 1840, Dubois promised to complete the house, to build a kitchen at the rear and a stable for at least four horses, and to enclose the property with a wall. The French chargé was to meet all expenses in finishing the house and would be allowed to occupy it until April 1, 1842. In return Odin paid him $6,500, a handsome profit on his original investment of $1,000.[38]

The site Dubois selected for his house was on the crest of a hill. From this vantage point one could look west toward town or south toward the Colorado River, which was about a mile away. The latter view must have struck Dubois as especially picturesque; one writer in 1848 described it as a "lovely valley," which by then was dotted "with small farms in a high state of cultivation, on which the neat and comfortable cottage of the husbandman

The Capitol of the Republic of Texas, Houston.Constructed in 1837. Thomas William Ward, architect. *Courtesy Barker Texas History Center.* The similarity between the Capitol at Houston and the French Legation suggests that the builder of the Capitol, Thomas William Ward, may have given Dubois de Saligny advice on the construction of his house. Ward was a prominent citizen of Austin from its earliest days.

French Government House. Engraving after a drawing by Julia Robertson. From the Galveston *Daily News,* February 9, 1896. *Courtesy Rosenberg Library, Galveston.* The gallery, the paired columns, the hipped roof, and the dormer windows of the French Legation are features which can also be found in the French-influenced architecture of Louisiana.

rears its humble roof." Although buildings and trees have long obscured this view to the river, at least one view from the Legation porch is legally protected: in 1985 the Austin City Council placed the view of the State Capitol from the porch of the Legation on a list of protected Capitol views.[39]

Although Dubois chose the site of his house, he had no experience in architecture and most probably needed assistance in its design. Such assistance may have come from Thomas William Ward, a public servant who had also worked as a builder in Louisiana. A native of Ireland, Ward attended the "military seminary" of the East India Company, but rather than become a cog in the British Empire he decided to become his own man in the New World. He worked for several years as a builder in New Orleans, but in 1835 he came to Texas in the volunteer outfit known as the New Orleans Grays. They fought at the Siege of

Bexar—that is, San Antonio—where Ward lost his right leg. After Texas won its independence, he was back in New Orleans, but in 1837 Augustus Chapman Allen recruited him to build the Capitol of the Republic of Texas at Houston. The Capitol reflected Ward's Louisiana experience in its two-story gallery with box columns, its hipped roof, and its dormer windows. When Edwin Waller, the first mayor of Austin, resigned that post in 1840, Ward was elected in his place. In that same year Ward lost his right arm while loading a cannon for a Texas Independence Day celebration. In 1841 David G. Burnet appointed Ward commissioner of the General Land Office, a post he held until 1853, when U.S. President Franklin Pierce appointed him Consul to Panama.[40]

The presence of Ward as a design consultant helps to explain the interesting blend of Anglo and Louisiana French features on the French Legation. Ward was an Anglo-American, but with years of experience with the Anglo-French building tradition of Louisiana. Thus, the Legation has a typically Anglo central hall plan, but also features found in Louisiana, such as French doors that open onto the gallery and a hipped roof—one that slopes down on all four sides—that sweeps out in front to cover the porch. The gallery itself is common to Anglo, French, and indeed *any* architecture in a sultry climate; the Doric piers on this gallery are paired in a manner reminiscent of many Louisiana houses and some of the greatest monuments of French classical architecture, such as the Galerie du Louvre in Paris. Such paired columns are unusual in the Anglo-American Greek Revival, as are the dormer windows. These dormers, the hipped roof, and the gallery give the Legation an appearance strikingly similar to Ward's Capitol. Ward is said to have purchased Dubois's sofa, armchair, and settees when the Legation was closed, but perhaps they were a gift—a token of appreciation for Ward's contribution to the design of the house.[41]

The framework of the Legation is hand-hewn cedar, probably found on or near the construction site, as was typical of the early log cabins of Austin. All visible surfaces, however, consist of machine-milled pine from the forests near Bastrop, some thirty miles to the east. It is the variety known as loblolly pine, com-

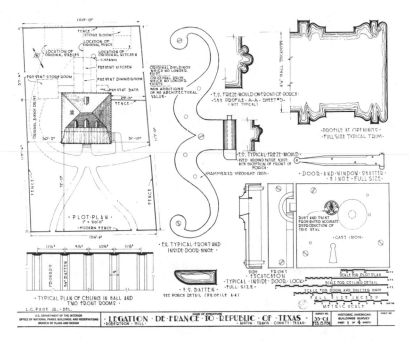

The French Legation, plot plan and architectural details. Historic American Buildings Survey drawing by L. C. Page, Jr., 1934. *Courtesy Library of Congress.* This 1934 HABS drawing includes a plot plan showing the probable location of the original kitchen and stables, as well as the location of the dining room, kitchen, and bath room added by the Robertsons. Also shown are a ram's head hinge and the lock from the front door.

monly found throughout the southern United States; the forests near Bastrop are noteworthy as the southwesternmost concentration. The lumber for the Legation would have come from one of the two steam-powered sawmills, the Austin City or the Copperas Creek mill, which were in operation near Bastrop by the fall of 1840. The Austin City Steam Mill had been operating for a year and probably provided the siding for the most important buildings in Austin, such as the Capitol and the President's House; this siding distinguished the French Legation from the log cabins in which most early Austinites lived and worked.[42]

17

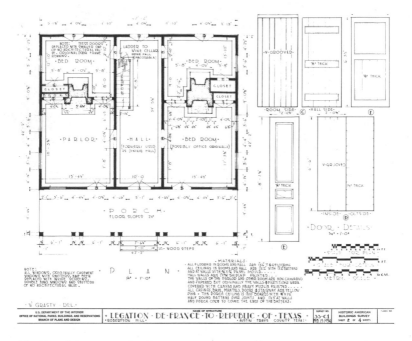

The French Legation, plan. Historic American Buildings Survey drawing by W. Grasty, 1934. *Courtesy Library of Congress.* This floor plan reflects the Robertson's usage of the rooms; most likely Dubois de Saligny would have used the two front rooms as a parlor and a dining room, and the two rear rooms as a study and a bed chamber.

Although the lumber for the Legation was homegrown, there was no local source of glass or paints and probably only one or two blacksmiths to provide hardware.One enterprising craftsman, L. F. Marguerat, advertised himself in the Austin *City Gazette* of February 3, 1841, as an "ornamental and house painter," claiming that he would "soon be receiving a large stock of paints, oils, turpentine, glass, and every other material necessary for his business." This shipment probably came from Galveston, the bustling Texas port of entry, but could have originated in New Orleans or even farther afield. For example, the S-shaped "ram's head" hinges on many of the doors at the Legation are typical of the hinges found in the Creole sections of New Orleans. If Marguerat worked on the Legation, he most likely provided the hinges, glazed all the windows, and painted the interior and exterior.[43]

The plan of the Legation—two rooms on each side of a central hall—is typical of much Anglo-American architecture and could be found in many other early Texas houses. The use of wood for the siding in the hall suggests the sort of open passageway known as a dogtrot, although the hall always seems to have been enclosed. Having recently been through a series of trying encounters with Bullock's pigs, Dubois would not have approved of a dogtrot in his house; if the carpenters who built the Legation had

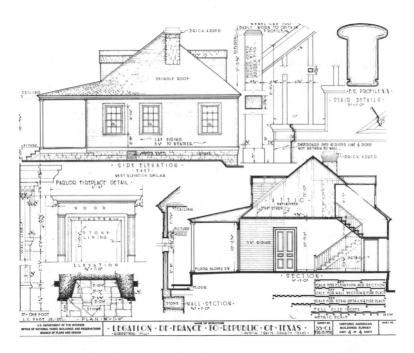

The French Legation, parlor fireplace. Historic American Buildings Survey drawing by L. C. Page, Jr., 1934. *Courtesy Library of Congress.* The mantels in the two front rooms are much finer than those in the typical Creole cottage; those in the French Legation possess the refinement and classical restraint of the Federal Style, popular in the United States in the first quarter of the nineteenth century.

one in mind, Dubois certainly insisted on a proper front door. Yet the hall did retain its wooden siding, suggesting that it was a reflex action, a case of the carpenters having built one dogtrot too many.

The carpenters who built the French Legation apparently owned a copy of *The American Builder's Companion* by the New England architect Asher Benjamin.This book and others like it were extremely popular with American carpenters, because they showed how to measure and make classical details. Indeed, the illustrations in this volume may have inspired the finest interior feature of the Legation, the pair of mantels in the two front rooms. Benjamin's plate 37 showed designs for three simple and elegant "chimney pieces," and plate 21 showed a design for a Doric cornice.The Legation carpenters took it from there, creating mantels that were not copied from any one plate in Benjamin's book, but captured the classical spirit he advocated. They must have spent more time on these than on any other interior feature; as a result, the mantels are finer than those in the Creole suburbs of New Orleans or in the homes of early Texas. Even Dubois must have been impressed, though he did not feel the need for such time-consuming details in the two rear rooms These were not public rooms, and their mantels consist of a few planks applied to the wall. Indeed, the simpler mantels may have been a result of Dubois attempting to finish the house as cheaply as possible after its sale to Odin.[44]

The walls of the four principal rooms were covered with canvas, which was simply tacked to the wooden frame of the house. The walls of the parlor were painted pale green, the hall yellow with bright pink trim, and the rest of the rooms various shades of pink. At the time of the restoration in the 1950s, sheetrock was placed between the studs in the wall, new canvas was installed, and it was painted in accordance with the research of Thomas Dunsford, an expert from Pittsburg Plate Glass Company.[45]

It is certain that Dubois conceived of his house as the setting for his fabulous dinner parties. The tall double doors that connect the two front rooms and the hall created a suite of rooms for entertaining, probably consisting of a parlor, hall, and dining room. Thus, the parlor and dining room would possess the beautifully carved mantels, the most attractive features of the interior. The two back rooms are smaller and better suited for more intimate purposes, such as a study and a bedroom.

The stairway leads from the hall to the upper floor. Its landing is the most awkward aspect of the design of the Legation, because it drastically shortens the ceiling and the doors opening into the back rooms and to the outside. The upstairs room, which receives light from three dormer windows, was most likely to have been the living quarters of Pluyette and Baudin. The long rectangular notches in the two posts have led to speculation that the servants slept in a hammock tied to the posts. Given that Dubois stayed there briefly and his servants stayed for a year, keeping an eye on things, it is more than likely that they slept downstairs.

The original kitchen was a completely separate building to the northeast of the house. Approximately seventeen by thirty feet, the roofline and long sides of the building ran north to south. The door was on the south side and opened into the kitchen itself; this room was dominated by the stone fireplace on the east wall. A door on the north wall led into the pantry that, like the kitchen, originally had a dirt floor. Apparently all of the cooking was done in the fireplace. Most of the utensils chef Charles Baudin used for cooking probably came from New Orleans.[46]

To the northwest of the house was a stable, which was roughly fifteen by twenty feet. Dubois owned several horses and most likely would have required a large stable, but it is doubtful that construction began before the charge left for New Orleans. In his agreement with Odin, Dubois promised to build a stable for three or four horses, and he probably provided for the most rudimentary sort of stable.[47]

Did Dubois de Saligny ever live in the Legation? The available historical evidence does not provide a definitive answer, but the house is nevertheless significant because Dubois had it built. It is important because of the other historical figures who stayed or dined there: Henri Castro, Sam Houston, Anson Jones.It is significant as the oldest remaining structure in Austin—more than a decade older than the great Greek Revival mansions of the 1850s—and as one of the limited number of buildings statewide that remain from the time when Texas was a republic.

The *Texas Sentinel* (Austin) of August 19, 1841, provides the first piece of solid evidence that the house was completed. Eugene Pluyette, that gentleman's gentleman and terror of pigs, informed the paper that the chargé's "house in this city has been newly fitted up of late, and furnished with costly furniture, wines, provisions, etc., in readiness for his reception, in the event of General Houston's election." What Dubois did not anticipate was that his friend General Houston would move the capital away from Austin.[49]

Pluyette also showed the house to Anson Jones, who had been out of town since March. Jones reported to his wife in a letter of November 10, 1841: "Our old friend Mr. Saligny has his house finished and furnished in almost regal magnificence." This suggests that the house was finished after Jones left in March, which would leave precious little time for Dubois to have lived in it. Jones went on to say that the "new furniture is Parisian and beautiful, the colors are orange, damask and gold." Whatever Parisian furniture Dubois sent to Austin was apparently removed, because the chair and sofa still in the Legation seem to have been made in New Orleans. Pluyette and Baudin undoubtedly enjoyed using Dubois's fine furniture and probably had a fine wine or two at their master's expense.[50]

Dubois probably did not begrudge his servants the use of his house, but he did become annoyed when Henri Castro stayed there. Castro was an advocate of French colonization, and he succeeded in persuading the Texas government to allow him to found several French communities west of San Antonio, including Castroville. Dubois initially supported his efforts, writing letters of introduction to influential men in Austin and even inviting him "to accept the hospitality of the mansion of the Legation in Austin, to live there during his entire stay in that town, and to make himself at home." That is exactly what Castro did upon his arrival on January 29, 1842. He gave several dinner parties attended by President Sam Houston, Secretary of State

Anson Jones, and even such a bitter enemy of Dubois as James Mayfield. To Dubois, his enemy was France's enemy, and he bitterly denounced Castro's motives in a letter to the foreign minister. Castro seems to have stayed at "the mansion of the Legation" for several weeks before returning to France.[51]

Soon after this Sam Houston began to move the Texas government to Houston; to make matters worse, a contingent of Mexican troops had invaded Texas. Rumors flew that the Mexican army had occupied San Antonio and that Austin was next on the agenda. Eugene Pluyette was as concerned as the next Austinite; as a precaution, he flew the French flag to ward off any Mexican troops who might enter the town. Rather than advancing to Austin, the troops returned to Mexico.[52]

On April 1, 1842, the agreement of occupancy between Dubois and Odin expired. Pluyette and Baudin must have sold some of the furniture and household goods and left for Galveston. They were certainly not alone in leaving town, because the removal of the government had resulted in a mass exodus. Thus, Father Odin was stuck with the nicest house in a ghost town. He knew that "it would be impossible to rent it at present, as more than half the population has left the town." He therefore put the house "under the care of a good family," rent-free. Even this incentive could not keep the house occupied. When William Bollaert visited Austin in August of 1843, "dreariness and desolation presented themselves; few houses appeared inhabited and many falling to decay. The 'Legation of France' empty, its doors and windows open, palings broken down and appearing as if it would soon be in ruins."[53]

Finally, on October 30, 1847, Odin sold the house and land to Moseley Baker, a hero of the Texas Revolution. Odin received $2,000, considerably less than the $6,500 he had paid for it six years earlier. Moseley Baker held the property only briefly. On May 16, 1848, he sold it to Dr. Joseph W. Robertson. Along with Captain James G. Swisher and some other leading citizens of Austin, Dr. Robertson hoped to found a girl's school, the Colorado Female Academy, run by C. W. Howell and his wife Maria. They proposed, in advertisements in the *Texas Democrat* (Austin) of August 16 and 30, 1848, to educate young ladies from primary school through college. Apparently Mrs. Howell felt intensely the isolation of the location—the college lasted only a semester or two. The first eight years of the house's existence were precarious, but when the Robertsons moved there sometime in 1849, a new era of stability and loving care for the house began.[54]

3.
THE ROBERTSON ERA

JOSEPH W. ROBERTSON AND HIS WIFE, Lydia Lee Robertson, were Austin pioneers. Joseph Robertson was born in South Carolina in 1809, attended Transylvania University in Lexington, Kentucky, and then practiced medicine for a year in Alabama. There he married Ann Philips, by whom he had two children, John and Elizabeth. He came alone to Texas in 1836; having found a place to live between Bastrop and the future site of Austin, he returned with his family the next year. Dr. Robertson represented Bastrop County in the Fourth Congress of the Republic of Texas (1839–40), which created Travis County out of part of Bastrop County. The Robertson family later moved to Austin, the county seat of Travis County, and Dr. Robertson opened a pharmacy on Congress Avenue in 1841. But in June of that year, Ann Philips died and was soon followed by her daughter Elizabeth. Dr. Robertson was left a widower with a young son.[55]

His second wife, Lydia Lee, was born in 1820 in Cincinnati, Ohio, then the largest city in the American West. In 1840, perhaps

The Joseph and Lydia Robertson family, a detail from a painting of the Capitol of the Republic of Texas by Julia Robertson, c. 1860. *Courtesy Barker Texas History Center*. In her painting of the 1839 Capitol, Julia Robertson included this portrait of her family riding in a covered wagon pulled by a pair of oxen.

seeking adventure on the frontier, Lydia, her sister Julia, and their brothers Joseph and John moved to Austin. The Lee sisters were beautiful and talented, skilled in the arts of drawing and signing. Mirabeau B. Lamar was inspired to write a poem to Lydia, and the Lee sisters' singing drew the praise of their next-door neighbor on Pecan Street, Alphonse Dubois de Saligny. The Lee family remained in Austin even after the capital was removed to Washington-on-the-Brazos; on September 7, 1842, Lydia gave her hand in marriage to Joseph Robertson.[56]

In 1843, Dr. Robertson was called upon to serve as the fifth mayor of Austin, and he and Lydia had the first of their ten children. Counting John, Dr. Robertson's son by his first marriage, the household grew to include five boys and six girls. The first four children were born in the Robertson House on Pecan Street. Among these was Julia Robertson, whose talent for painting is evident in the view of the Legation still in the house. Sarah was the first child to be born in the Legation, in 1850, and she was the last person to die there, in 1940. Her younger sister Lydia was born in the house in 1855 and lived there continuously until her death in 1939.[57]

The French Legation, by Julia Robertson, c. 1858. Oil on canvas, 15 ¹/₄ x 19 ¹/₄ in. *Courtesy French Legation Committee, Daughters of the Republic of Texas.* Julia Robertson's painting of the house, said to have been done when she was twelve, shows how it sat alone on its hilltop in 1858. The painting still hangs in the French Legation.

When the Robertsons bought the house in 1848, the hill on which it rested became known as Robertson Hill. In those days the house must have been filled with the joyful noise of a large and growing family. Joseph and Lydia took the front room on the right as their bedroom, because there was no other place for their large canopy bed, chest of drawers, and nightstand. Both of the back rooms became bedrooms, which must have become quite crowded by 1862, when the last child, Thomas William, was born. It is likely that trundle beds were kept beneath the regular beds; even with this expedient the children must have had to double or triple up. Possibly the older boys slept upstairs, even though that room remained an unfinished attic until the 1950s. The center of the household, though, was the hall, which served as the living room and also as the place of family meals.

The only changes made to the house during Dr. Robertson's lifetime were a lattice attached to the columns on the west side of the front porch and an additional room on the east side of the kitchen. This room, which shared the large stone hearth with the kitchen, was for Maria, the black woman who cooked for the family and nursed the children. Slave's quarters were built further north on the property, and a spring house was placed to the northwest near a spring that has now run dry.[58]

Dr. Joseph Robertson died early in August 1870, and was buried on August 9. The *Daily Austin Republican* reported that "the funeral of our esteemed townsman. . . . was in keeping with his life and character. There was no ostentation, no pomp." Among the pall-bearers were General W. P. Hardeman, Judge John B. Costas, and Colonel Sterling C. Robertson. The *Republican* observed that they were "*all old Texans*, who walked beside the

The French Legation, aerial view, 1873. Detail from *Bird's Eye View of the City of Austin Travis County Texas*, by Augustus Koch, 1873. Lithograph, 19 ³/₄ x 28 ¹/₂ in. *Courtesy Austin History Center, Austin Public Library*. An 1873 aerial view reveals that the Legation was still one of the easternmost houses in Austin, and provides a clue as to the original location of the kitchen and stables.

The French Legation, 1880s Robertson addition. Photograph for the Historic American Buildings Survey by Louis C. Page, Jr., 1934. *Courtesy Library of Congress.* Architect Louis C. Page, Jr., snapped this, the only known photograph of the Robertson addition, which contained a dining room, a kitchen, and a bath room.

hearse with uncovered heads. Thus it is! they are 'passing away.'" With the death of Dr. Robertson, there remained only a few citizens of Austin who could remember the time when Austin had been the capital of the Republic of Texas.[59]

A fire destroyed the original kitchen around 1880. Mrs. Robertson decided to build a new dining room and kitchen onto the north side of the house. The back door of the house now opened into the dining room, and the northeast bedroom opened into a new bathroom. Between the dining room/kitchen and the bathroom was a narrow back porch that ran out to the cistern. This back porch was supported by four slender columns with typically Victorian detailing. No attempt was made to hide the fact that this was an add-on, but the white clapboard siding did blend with the original house. The roof of the addition rose only to the eaves of the house, leaving the original roof with its single dormer unchanged. Thus, the Robertsons made the eventual restoration of the house to its original appearance easy.

After the death of Mrs. Robertson in 1902, her daughter Lillie continued to live in the house. Lillie was an early member of the William B. Travis chapter of the Daughters of the Republic of Texas, to which she devoted much of her time. Lillie saw to it that the nearby State Cemetery was well cared for and with her friend Emma Kyle Burleson was on the committee that transferred the DRT's collection of artifacts from the Capitol to the new DRT Museum on the second floor of the historic Land Office Building. Lillie also served as an early tour guide for her house, which, like many people, she called the "French Embassy." In this, as in other cases, Lillie's enthusiasm and pride over the house carried her away. She would repeat to visitors the old legends that many parts of the house had been imported from France: locks, hinges,

The French Legation in 1934. Photograph for the Historic American Buildings Survey by Louis C. Page, Jr., 1934. *Couresy Library of Congress.* This photograph shows the house when it was occupied by Miss Lillie Robertson. Note the lattice-work on the west (left) side of the porch, and the absence of the balustrade visible in Julia Robertson's drawing (page 15) and painting (page 26).

mantels, windows, even the front door! None of this was true, but Lillie Robertson performed an invaluable service not only in maintaining the house but also in keeping this historic building in the memory of the public.[60]

A more official form of recognition came in September, 1934, when a young architect named Louis C. Page, Jr., visited the house. He and Louis F. Southerland had attempted to start an architectural practice in Tyler in 1932, but the Great Depression killed off the fledgling firm. Now Page was working for the federal government under one of Franklin D. Roosevelt's Works Progress Administration projects, the Historic American Buildings Survey. Page took photographs of the house and made several beautiful drawings, recording front and side elevations, the floor plan, a section (a cut-away view), and many details of the building's construction. The French Legation was thus among the first buildings listed in the Historic American Buildings Survey, and Page's drawings of the house are preserved in the Library of Congress in Washington, D.C. The year after his visit to the Legation, Page and Southerland began to practice architecture in Austin, and their firm became—-and remains—the largest in the city.[61]

Lillie was later joined in the house by her older sister Sarah Robertson Smith, after the death of her husband Robert A. Smith in 1932. Lillie passed away in 1939 in the canopy bed in the master bedroom, the same room and the same bed in which she had been born in 1855. Sarah outlived her by little more than six months, dying in May, 1940. She was the last person to live in the house and the Robertsons' occupancy of the old French Legation ended with her passing.

4.
RESTORING THE HOUSE

THE DAUGHTERS OF THE REPUBLIC OF TEXAS had long been associated with the French Legation, thanks to one of their number, Lillie Robertson. The organization was founded by Betty Ballinger and Holly Bryan Perry in 1891 as the Daughters of the Lone Star Republic; at the first annual meeting in 1892, the name was changed to the Daughters of the Republic of Texas. As their first president the Daughters elected Mrs. Anson Jones, widow of the last president of the Republic of Texas. The objectives of the organization were—and still are—"to perpetuate the memory and spirit of the men and women who achieved and maintained the Independence of Texas," to encourage historical research and publication on the Republic of Texas, and to promote the celebration of Texas Independence Day (March 2) and San Jacinto Day (April 21), which commemorates the battle in which the Texan army defeated the Mexican forces under General Antonio Lopez de Santa Anna. Many Daughters were active in collecting artifacts from the era of the Republic of Texas; starting in 1903, some of these were displayed in a room in the State Capitol. These artifacts became the nucleus of the DRT Museum, which occupies the second floor of the historic Land Office Building just southeast of the Capitol. In 1905, the DRT became the custodian of the Alamo, the greatest shrine of Texas independence. Thus, there was ample reason to think that the Daughters might take on the task of restoring the French Legation.[62]

The Daughters attempted to raise funds to purchase the house, but were unsuccessful.Undaunted, DRT members Mrs. Paul Goldman and Jane Oliphant Webb, wife of the eminent historian Walter Prescott Webb, turned to the state legislature for help. In May, 1945, the legislature passed a bill authorizing the use of $24,256.16 left over from the Texas Centennial celebration of 1936 for the purchase of the "French Embassy." This money, however, was from the federal government's contribution to the Centennial fund, and it was unclear that the state had the right to appropriate it. Not until 1947 did Texas Attorney General Price Daniel rule that the Centennial funds could be used to buy the Legation. Even this did not guarantee that the state would buy the house, because the Robertson heirs believed that the property was worth considerably more than $24,000 and that they could find a private buyer. But the memory of Miss Lillie and a sense of duty prevailed, and the Robertsons sold the Legation on August 11, 1948, for not one penny more than the state had first offered.[63]

The restoration of the Legation got off to an extremely slow start. The DRT did not take possession of the property until August of 1949, and the Board of Management did not create a French Legation Committee until 1950. This committee was chaired by Mrs. Henry R. Wofford, president-general of the DRT, and its members included Mrs. George S. (Ouida) Nalle, daughter of Texas governors James and Miriam Ferguson, and Mrs. Carl (Paula) Stautz, whose husband, an architect, donated his services to the Legation. At the same time, the Violet Crown Garden Club of Austin, under the direction of Mrs. T. J. Holbrook and Mrs. Frank Davol, began to plan the restoration of the gardens. Not until 1953, however, were plans drawn and work begun.[64]

The earliest plan for restoration of the house and its gardens was the work of Carl Stautz and Armon E. Mabry, two Austin architects, and James Dalrymple, a graduate student in landscape architecture at Texas A&M University. Their plan for the grounds was only partially executed, but they had a significant impact on the appearance of the French Legation Museum. They conceived of a grassy "mall" leading from San Marcos Street toward the house, on either side of which was a "bosque," or wooded area.

The mall ended at a set of stone steps up to a terrace garden. From the steps to the east side of the house there were flower beds laid out in the French formal style. Similar flower beds on a smaller scale were planted on the west side of the house. To the south and southeast were open, grassy lawns, with gravel paths allowing for various circuits around the formal gardens and front lawn. As lovely as these gardens are, it must be remembered that they are a creation of the 1950s, in no sense a restoration of an original scheme.[65]

This plan virtually presumed the demolition of the Robertson kitchen and the reconstruction of the original kitchen and stables. These would be placed to the north of the house, creating an entrance court, which would serve as the main entry to the museum. The proposed outbuildings were in the same area as the original ones, but Stautz and Mabry apparently could not resist the temptation to improve upon the original. The kitchen and stable were to be precisely the same size, with neatly hipped roofs, and with geometrically shaped herb gardens on the north and south side of each building. Like the garden plan, this scheme was very attractive but not very accurate; there is no evidence that Dubois intended such a formal arrangement for his outbuildings.

In 1953, Armon Mabry and James Dalrymple left Austin and were thus unable to continue work at the Legation. An Austin landscape architect, C. Coatsworth Pinkney, agreed to donate his services to the Legation, improving on the earlier plan and bringing it to life. A native of Denver and a graduate of Harvard in landscape architecture, Pinkney had worked as an assistant to Arthur Shurtleff, who designed the gardens at Colonial Williamsburg, and to Morley J. Williams, who worked at Mount Vernon and Stratford. Pinkney put his own stamp on the original plan in a number of ways. He decided against planting the "bosque" to the north and south of the mall, leaving open the gently rolling grounds. He redesigned the steps to the terrace, replacing the rather cramped pair of steps shown in the plan with an elegant three-stage composition. The formal flower beds he turned into mazelike miniature hedges. He planted the crepe myrtles that every summer turn the mall into a dazzling display

The French Legation, Austin. Photograph by Todd Webb, 1964–1967. *Courtesy Amon Carter Museum.* In the 1950s the Daughters of the Republic of Texas restored the house and landscaped the grounds. Architect Raiford Stripling restored the balustrade shown by Julia Robertson (pages 15 and 26), and added a panel reading "Legation de France." This photograph was taken by Todd Webb for the book *Texas Homes of the Nineteenth Century.*

of pink blossoms and specified many other plants and trees, including the redbud, the rose of Sharon, the camellia, the mountain laurel, and the lantana, which grace the grounds.[66]

Carl Stautz devoted most of his efforts to research on the restoration of the house, but the actual specifications for the house were written by another Austin architect, A. Watt Harris, in 1953. The only major external change was the removal of the lattice that the Robertsons had added in the late nineteenth century. Inside, the changes were more extensive. The chimneys and fireplaces were repaired, and the house was wired for electricity—apparently for the first time! New casement windows, with older panes of glass whenever possible, replaced the sash windows from the Robertson era. The hinges on the windows were copied from those on the front door and elsewhere in the house. The outside blinds were installed at this time. Also, a brick terrace was built across the north side of the house, even though no such terrace ever existed—brick was not available in Austin in the early 1840s.[67]

In order to restore the house to its appearance in the days of the Republic, the Robertson addition to the house was removed. It was said to be in "dilapidated condition," although some lumber salvaged from it was used to build a caretaker's house on the northwest corner of the property. The decision to demolish the Victorian addition was in keeping with the preservation philosophy of the 1950s, in which the objective was to return a building to its earliest appearance. In the 1980s, preservationists would contend that subsequent additions to a house are also historic and should be preserved, but the DRT acted in accordance with contemporary standards.[68]

The Daughters also consulted with Carlton Safford and Rudolph Hendric, interior decorators from West Granville, Massachusetts. After a visit to Austin in October of 1954, Rudy Hendric made several quick sketches and a written report. From paint scrapings taken from the rooms he concluded that all the rooms had been painted in "a soft warm French grey," except for the hall, which he thought had been "oyster white." He urged the Daughters to accept no furniture made later than 1840 and to use mainly Empire furniture with a few pieces of Louis XVI. Hendric also suggested several fabrics for curtains from Scalamandre Silks, Inc., of New York City. Scalamandre silk was eventually used for the draperies—though it is highly unlikely that Dubois brought anything so fine to Austin—but Safford and Hendric were not retained.[69]

In May, 1955, Mrs. Barclay (Margaret) Megarity of Waco became president-general of the DRT. Mrs. Megarity ran for president pledging to complete the restoration of the Legation. She raised substantial funds for the project and saw it to completion during her two-year term. Her most important decision was to involve Raiford Stripling of San Augustine in the project. Stripling was an architect specializing in the restoration of historic buildings and had been responsible for reconstructing Mission Espiritu Santo in Goliad and for restoring the Ezekiel Cullen House in San Augustine, which in 1953 became the headquarters of the Ezekiel Cullen chapter of the DRT. Mrs. Megarity also requested that an expert from the Pittsburg Plate Glass Company, Thomas Dunsford, examine the original canvas to determine the colors used in each room scientifically.[70]

Architect Stripling and the contractor, Louis Runnels—both members of the Sons of the Republic of Texas—began work on the Legation in November, 1955, and finished in time for the opening of the museum on April 6, 1956. Stripling replaced the canvas covering on the walls and painted it according to the Dunsford report; sheetrock was placed between the studs for extra insulation. The attic was also insulated and sealed, and a powder room was installed. On the roof of the porch, just in front of the dormer windows, Stripling added a balustrade, in the middle of which is a panel reading "Legation de France."

Both Stripling and Mrs. Megarity were acutely aware that mistakes had been made in the earlier phases of the restoration. Particularly troubling was the brick terrace added to the rear of the house. More subtly erroneous were the new windows: an original casement window discovered in the attic had four panes and opened outward, whereas the 1953 version had three panes and opened inward. Mrs. Megarity and the DRT planned to correct these errors "when money is more plentiful," but that day has not yet come.[71]

While the restoration was drawing near completion, plans for the decoration of the house moved forward. Silk curtains from Scalamandre of New York were installed in each of the rooms. The National Society of Colonial Dames of America, led by Mrs. Ben Powell of Austin, assisted in the furnishing of the parlor. Mrs. Powell herself donated the bronze sculpture of the Marquis de Lafayette and its pedestal, the Wedgwood bowl, and the rosewood stool. Mrs. Megarity and Miss Pauline Breustedt donated a Louis XV armchair, which in 1985 was reupholstered in apricot-

The French Legation, kitchen, 1966. Photograph by the author. Raiford
Stripling returned to Austin in 1966 to build the commodious kitchen which,
like the original, was a completely separate building.

colored velvet that Mrs. Megarity acquired in Europe. Miss
Emma Kyle Burleson, a member of the DRT and a close friend of
Lillie Robertson, had given an armchair belonging to Dubois to
Lillie and the matching sofa to the DRT Museum. With the
opening of the French Legation Museum, these two remaining
pieces of the original furnishings were reunited. In 1985, Mrs.
Megarity donated the beautiful damask material used to recover
Dubois's sofa.[72]

Ten years after the French Legation Museum opened, Raiford
Stripling returned to Austin to reconstruct the original kitchen.
The entire project was funded by Mr. and Mrs. John Ward Beretta
of San Antonio, including an archaeological dig in May and June
of 1966, in which the Texas Archeological Research Laboratory
from the University of Texas uncovered the stone foundations of
the original hearth. (The archaeologists also discovered that

Indians had used the site for thousands of years, between 4000 B.C. and 1000 A.D.) The report also suggested that the original kitchen had a dirt floor, because artifacts were distributed evenly beneath the soil, whereas a hardwood floor would have left artifacts only around the periphery. The Berettas collected almost all of the French cooking antiques displayed in the kitchen and set up an endowment expressly for the purpose of maintaining the building and its artifacts. In 1975, Mrs. Megarity had an herb garden planted just north of the kitchen, in memory of her father.[73]

In 1974, a carriage house was constructed on the northeast corner of the grounds. Mrs. George P. Red, the president-general of the DRT from 1973 to 1975, obtained funds from the Houston Endowment and the Moody Foundation and oversaw the construction. John Ward Beretta was responsible for selecting the site of the building: while examining the 1873 Augustus Koch aerial view of Austin, which included the Robertson house, Beretta noticed another building off in the woods and concluded that this must have been the carriage house. Subsequent archaeological research suggests that the stable was actually in the northwest corner of the grounds. Raiford Stripling was again the architect; he designed a two-story building, far larger than most houses in 1840s Austin. The downstairs included two spacious stalls, a harness room (now used as a powder room), and a room to house a carriage. Originally the floor was dirt, but a new concrete floor was poured in 1981 when a gift shop and office were established. An upstairs room is used for the DRT French Legation Committee and is rented out for weddings and other social occasions.[74]

In the 1960s and 1970s, the DRT concentrated on recreating the kitchen and the carriage house, but in that period little maintenance was done on the house itself. By 1982, it was clear that the original building was in need of extensive repair. French Legation Committee chairwoman Mrs. George T. (Opal) Hollis, past president-general (1979–1981), and treasurer Mrs. Joe L. (Lois) Douglas, a member of the Reuben Hornsby Chapter-DRT and a great-granddaughter of Joseph and Lydia Robertson, successfully applied for preservation grants from the Texas Historical Commission and the Moody Foundation of Galveston. In 1983, Mrs. Joe L. (Lois) Douglas was appointed chairwoman by the DRT Board of Management. A flurry of activity began, much of it financed through a five-to-one matching challenge grant from Mrs. H. M. (Amanda) Amsler and the persuasive efforts of DRT president-general Mrs. Rex L. (Wanda) Arnold. A new sprinkler system was installed throughout the two and a half acres of the Legation grounds, a parking lot was constructed on state-owned property adjacent to the Legation compound, and extensive repairs were made to the buildings. All masonry joints in the foundation were repointed, the fireplaces and chimneys were repaired, the porch deck was removed and replaced with one made of cypress, the roof and dormers were extensively repaired, and approximately 30 percent of the boards on the exterior of the kitchen were replaced. The house, kitchen, and carriage house were all given a new coat of paint. Finally, in early 1987, portions of the canvas on the walls in the house were replaced, and the entire interior was repainted using the original color scheme.[75]

5.
THE CONTENTS
OF THE HOUSE

TWO PIECES OF FURNITURE IN THE HOUSE are said to remain from the days when it was the mansion of the French Legation, the sofa and armchair in the parlor. Miss Emma Kyle Burleson, a member of the Daughters of the Republic of Texas, donated the chair to Miss Lillie Robertson and the sofa to the DRT Museum in 1917. (The sofa returned to the Legation in 1956.) Miss Emma had

The French Legation, parlor. Photograph by the author. This sofa and armchair, said to have belonged to Dubois de Saligny, was probably made in New Orleans around 1840, and was later owned by Thomas William Ward.

purchased this furniture in 1907 from Virginia Wilson Spence, who came from an old Austin family. In a letter preserved in the Texas State Archives, Mrs. Spence explained that her father, Captain William McFarland Wilson, had bought these pieces from his good friend Colonel Thomas William Ward, who had purchased them from Dubois when Texas was admitted to statehood. Actually, Ward would have had to purchase them from Eugene Pluyette in April, 1842, the last Austin saw of the French Legation, but Mrs. Spence's letter contains convincing details. She wrote that her father bought the furniture when Colonel Ward was appointed U. S. consul to Panama; indeed, President Franklin Pierce did appoint Ward to this post in 1853. Moreover, the rosewood frames of the sofa and chair are of a type made in New Orleans in the 1840s. Dubois could certainly have purchased them while on his way to Texas or on one of his numerous visits. This simplified version of the Louis XV style must have appealed to his patriotism as well as to his taste.[76]

Also in the parlor is a handsome Empire-style clock owned by the Robertsons. The works of this clock are French, but its case is most likely American, dating to the 1840s. A Robertson family legend has it that Mrs. Robertson wanted this clock so badly that she traded her pony for it. The rest of the furnishings in the parlor were donated at the time of the restoration by the National Society of Colonial Dames of America Resident in the State of Texas. Most noteworthy is the Aubusson carpet, which was woven in the late eighteenth or early nineteenth century. The pianoforte—an early, smaller form of the piano—was made in London by Astor and Company and dates to around 1815. A Tennessee doctor, Elijah Sims, bought it for his daughter Martha, who brought it with her to Texas in 1857. The statue of the Marquis de Lafayette is the work of the French realist sculptor Aime-Jules Dalou. Originally intended to be part of a monument to be built at Versailles, this smaller version was cast in the years just after the sculptor's death in 1902.

The French Legation, the study. Photograph by the author. The English Regency wine cooler in the study is one of many nineteenth-century artifacts.

The French Legation, front bed room. Photograph by the author. The bed and dresser, made c. 1830, were owned by Joseph and Lydia Robertson, and have been in the house since 1848.

Most noteworthy in the study is the wine cooler, or cellaret, which is from the English Regency period (circa 1820). Made of oak and lined with lead, it was used to chill bottles of wine in cold spring water. The wine cooler, shaped like an ancient sarcophagus, reflects the European and American fascination with the classical era of Greece and Rome. Also of note is the table—actually a dressing table without its mirror—made in New Orleans in the 1840s. On the upper portion of each curving cabriole leg is carved the face of a man with a long, flowing beard. The book press on the bookshelf was donated by a man who theorized that Dubois had used it to print his own Republic of Texas money. There is, however, no evidence that Dubois ever printed his own money; moreover, this particular book press dates only to the late nineteenth century and could not possibly have been owned by Dubois.

In the hall are several works of art on French or Franco-American themes. A large colored engraving depicts Benjamin

Franklin at the court of Louis XVI and Marie Antoinette in 1778. This was printed at Philadelphia in 1853 and was based on a painting by Baron Jolly now in the Philadelphia Museum of Art. The pair of engravings on the east wall depict the marriage of the Dauphin Louis XV to Maria Terese, the Infanta of Spain, in the Royal Chapel at the Palace of Versailles and the grand ball that ensued. Charles Nicholas Cochin the younger (1715–90) designed both prints and engraved the former; his father, Charles Nicholas Cochin the elder (1688–1754), engraved the latter. The set of six plates are Sevres porcelain made for the Chateau de Tuileries during the reign of Louis Philippe, around 1840. On each plate two cherubs flank a wreath, inside of which is a crown and an intertwined L and P, the insignia of King Louis Philippe.

The remaining rooms of the house contain mostly Robertson furniture and demonstrate how the taste of a Victorian family

The French Legation, the rear bed room. Photograph by the author. The rear bed room was quite probably used by Dubois de Saligny as his own bedchamber. The Robertsons used it as a children's bed room. A trundle bed would have been kept under the c. 1860 spindle-post bed. Julia Robertson's painting of the house hangs on the wall.

The French Legation, kitchen interior. Photograph by the author. The kitchen is stocked with cooking utensils collected in France and New Orleans.

changed over the decades. The oldest furniture is in the front bedroom. The great canopy bed, made of walnut and pine, was Dr. Robertson's; he may have bought it in Lexington, Kentucky, where he attended Transylvania University in the 1820s. According to Robertson family reminiscences, Lydia Lee brought the dresser and nightstand all the way from Cincinnati. Certainly brought from Ohio was the portrait of Lydia's brother, Dr. Abram Lee. This self-portrait is most attractive and is unusual for the informal attire in which the artist depicts himself. Among the donated items in the front bedroom, the hearth screen stands out. This object was used to protect a sitter's face from the heat and sparks of the fire.

In the back bedroom is another Robertson bed, this one made around 1860. In contrast to the thick, sturdy, and simple posts of the older canopy bed, this one has more delicately proportioned and more decidedly ornamental spindle posts. Also in this room is a painting by one of the Robertson girls, Julia, said to have been

Dough box, panetier, and bread box. Photograph by the author. Several artifacts in the kitchen relate to breadmaking; the dough could rise unmolested in the dough box, and the simple, upright bread box and the cage-like panetier were for storing the finished products.

done when she was twelve years old. If this tradition is correct, the painting shows the house as it was in 1858. It is charming in its childlike naiveté, but is also an invaluable document as to the original appearance of the house. The earthenware toilet set is probably of German origin and was made around 1870. The set consists of a bowl and pitcher, a small pitcher, a toothbrush vase, a covered powder box, and a shaving cup.

Upstairs one finds a suite of Victorian bedroom furniture, which belonged to Sarah Robertson, who took it with her when she married Robert A. Smith at Ballinger, Texas. Joseph W. Hannig, a Prussian immigrant with a shop on Pecan Street, crafted this furniture in the Renaissance Revival style, a blend of classical and natural motifs. The walnut bed, for example, has both classical urn-shaped finials and carved acorns and foliage. The dresser and washstand have marble tops and walnut-acorn-and-leaf-handles. These three pieces date to the 1880s and constitute a dramatic shift from the simplicity of the earliest Robertson furniture.[77]

The French country kitchen displays many attractive artifacts in a variety of materials: wood, glass, ceramics, pewter, copper, brass, and iron. In the northeast corner are two items used in making bread. On the floor is a dough box, a simple rectangular box on legs, in which the flour and yeast was stored and in which the dough could rise. This piece dates to the late seventeenth or early eighteenth century. Above it is a panetier, or baker's safe, which dates to the early nineteenth century. Freshly baked bread could be kept under lock and key, and the bars allowed the bread to cool unmolested by the hands of children or the nose of the family dog.

The Legation kitchen has a large complement of copper pots, but the most interesting copper object is the bath warmer, which was made around 1800. This odd-looking contraption has an urnlike central section that holds hot coals and two upward-curving tubes that allow air to circulate and keep the embers glowing. The warmer was simply placed in a tub full of spring water and left there until the right temperature was reached.

Among ceramic items are plates from the town of Quimper, France, a nineteenth-century colander, and a set of dessert cups

Lacemaker's lamp and fly trap. Photograph by the author. The lacemaker's lamp maximized the light from a single candle. The fly trap lured unsuspecting insects up the chimney with molasses or other sweet, sticky substances.

known as pot de creme. The large blue and white china bowl is from the Ch'ing Dynasty, reign of Yung Cheng (1723–35). The style is strongly reminiscent of the Ming Dynasty, reign of Hsuan Te, which was in great demand in eighteenth-century Europe. Indeed, the Chinese may have intended this bowl for European export.

Pewter, an alloy of lead and tin, was very popular in the eighteenth and nineteenth centuries. In the Legation's collection are a saliere (a two-chambered box to hold salt and pepper), two pitchers for mulled wine or hot chocolate, a bed warmer, and a soup tureen in the rococo style characteristic of the Strasbourg area of France. Near the door is a lavabo, a pewter font with a brass spigot, used to wash before cooking.

On the table is a glass fly-trap. This teardrop-shaped object has a chimney in the bottom, which forms an O-shaped reservoir into which molasses, sugar water, or anything sweet and sticky can be poured. Thanks to the tiny legs on which the trap rests, flies can crawl up the chimney, only to get stuck inside. Next to the fly-trap is a lace-maker's lamp. Water was poured into the bowl atop a long stem, and a candle was placed next to it. The combination of glass and water magnified the light from the candle.

Near the hearth are many iron items, including a pair of irons for pressing clothes and a waffle iron. The names of both these objects survived long after they ceased to be made of iron. An early toaster consists of supports to hold up a piece of bread near the open fire, set on a swivel so that the bread can be turned.

The tall clock was made in the area of France known as Morbier more than 150 years ago. It runs by a system of weights and must be wound once a week. The great pendulum is made of brass, and the face is made of porcelain, which is why it is still gleaming after some 150 years.

Easy to overlook amidst all the fascinating items in the kitchen is the pair of French sideboards on which many of the artifacts sit. The buffet on the south wall is made of fruitwood and dates to the mid-eighteenth century; the buffet on the north wall is made of cherry and dates to the early nineteenth century. Both are of provincial origin and possess that straightforward and simple dignity so characteristic of many country pieces.

NOTES

¹The standard scholarly work on Dubois de Saligny and the French Legation is Nancy Nichols Barker, ed., *The French Legation in Texas* (Austin: Texas State Historical Association, 1971 and 1973). For Dubois's mission of exploration, see I, 39–103; quotation on p. 103.

²The best review of Dubois's life is in the introduction to ibid., I, 17-35. His birth certificate, showing him to have been of bourgeois origin, is reproduced on p. 81.

³Ibid., I. 21. In the deed by which he purchased twenty-one acres from Anson Jones and sold the same to John Mary Odin, Dubois referred to himself as "a count of the Kingdom of France" and "Knight of the Legion of Honor." Later, when he married in 1863, he declared himself "a Count of the Holy Empire," and his death certificate called him "a Roman count." However, no evidence has been uncovered that Dubois was of noble lineage or that he assumed a noble title; indeed, his birth certificate (Barker, *French Legation*, I, 81) shows his origins were common.

⁴Mary Starr Barkley, *History of Travis County and Austin, 1839–1899* (Waco: Texian Press, 1963), and Roxanne Kuter Williamson, *Austin, Texas: An American Architectural History* (San Antonio: Trinity University Press, 1973), 1-23.

⁵According to the Houston *Morning Star* of January 27, 1840, Dubois arrived with his secretary and two servants. No secretary is mentioned either in Dubois's correspondence or in secondary documentation, but apparently his name was Jules Dulong. The *Texas Sentinel* of October 24, 1840, stated that Dulong "was formerly connected with the legation, having resigned his situation on coming to this country." Dulong opened a general store, which had in stock French wines and champagnes. The servants were Eugene Pluyette, a butler, and Charles Baudin, a chef. Pluyette is well documented because of the Pig War: Richard Bullock to David G. Burnet. February 20, 1841, in Barker, *French Legation*, I, 213-216, and George P. Garrison, ed., *Diplomatic Correspondence of the Republic of Texas* (Washington, D.C.: 1908-1911), III, 1289, 1298, and 1334, which includes the testimony of Jules Dulong. Dubois never mentioned the name of his chef in his correspondence, but it was most likely Baudin. The *Texas Sentinel* of July 1, 1841, mentioned the

"French wines, Principe cegars, West Indian sweetmeats and lusty promises" served at Dubois's dinner table, and the *Sentinel* of July 7, 1841, mentions "brandy cherries." Thus, rum-flavored sweetmeats, brandied cherries, and other confections were the specialty of Dubois's chef. Apparently, after Dubois left town in April of 1841, Baudin went into business for himself, opening a confectionery shop on Congress Avenue. An advertisement in the Austin *City Gazette* of November 24, 1841, promised that "the public will always find a large assortment of Cakes of the best quality, Bonbons, and every variety of Candies."

⁶Dubois wrote from Houston on January 19, 1840, that he had arrived at Galveston on January 17 (Barker, *French Legation*, I, 115). He claimed to have arrived in Austin on January 30, but both the *Texas Sentinel* and the Austin *City Gazette* of February 5 say that he arrived on February 3. On February 19, 1840, the *Texas Sentinel* reported that he had left Austin the preceding Friday—February 14—but the diplomat wrote from Houston on March 17 that he had just left Austin on March 12. By March 30 he was in New Orleans, where he stayed until late May. Most of June he spent in Galveston, and he did not return to Austin until July 24, 1840 (Barker, *French Legation*, I, 129, 131, 144, 158).

⁷Dubois to Louis Adolphe Thiers, July 26, 1840, in Barker, *French Legation*, I, 158.

⁸Ibid., I, 160.

⁹The names of Dubois's slaves are listed in Richard Bullock's bill, appended to his letter to David G. Burnet, February 20, 1841, in ibid., I, 215; Dubois mentioned in a letter to Thiers, July 26, 1840, that a "female domestic that I had bought in New Orleans died yesterday after an illness of thirty-six hours caused by the hardships of the journey" (ibid., I, 160); that this domestic was named Flora is evident from Bullock's bill, which was copied for Dubois de Saligny to James Mayfield, in Garrison, *Diplomatic Correspondence*, III, 1305, which refers to "digging a grave and conveying Flora."

¹⁰On the counterfeit controversy, see the letters of James Harper Starr to James S. Mayfield, March 29, 1841, and James S. Mayfield to George S. McIntosh, May 12, 1841, and the affidavit of James Latham, July 31, 1840, all in Garrison, *Diplomatic Correspondence*, III, 1323–1329.

¹¹Dubois apparently arrived in Austin on July 24, 1840, and moved into his rented house on July 29. Barker, *French Legation*, I, 215. On Bullock's Inn, see Williamson, *Austin, Texas*, 17–20. The description of Dubois's rented house is in Frank Brown, "Annals of Travis County and of the City of Austin" (typescripts at the Austin History Center of the Austin Public Library and at the Archives in the Texas State Library), chapter VII, 28, 31, 32. Brown states that the site was later occupied by Mrs. E. B. Smith and Dr. Swearingen. The Swearingen residence (now demolished) was at 313 W. Sixth. Swearingen purchased the land from Caroline A. Brown and Sidney Brown on December 6, 1886; the Browns bought it from Mrs. Elizabeth B. Smith on December 11, 1874; Mrs. Smith bought it from James M. Long, assignee for Jesse Billingsley, on July 3, 1849; Billingsley was the original owner. See Deed Books at the Travis County Courthouse, Austin, vol. 71, p. 295, vol. 28, p. 289, and vol. C, p. 529, and Patent No. 261 at the Archives and Records,

General Land Office, Austin. On Billingsley, see Sam Houston Dixon and Louis Wiltz Kemp, *The Heroes of San Jacinto* (Houston: Anson Jones Press, 1932), 157–158. Frank Brown states that Dubois was still living on Pecan Street at the time of the pig incident (that is, February 19) *and* when he was attacked by Bullock (March 24). This leaves precious little time for Dubois to have lived in the mansion he was building, because he left town on April 29. For Dubois's characterization of his house as a "shanty," see Dubois to Thiers, June 26, 1840, in Barker, *French Legation*, I, 153.

[12]On Fathers Odin and Timon, see Ralph Francis Bayard, *Lone-Star Vanguard* (St. Louis: 1945). Father Bayard's account depicts Odin and Timon as staying at the present French Legation, but this supposition is not supported by the documents he cites. Odin's diary is excerpted in J. M. Kirwin, ed., *Diamond Jubilee 1847–1922 of the Diocese of Galveston and St. Mary's Cathedral* (Galveston: 1922); see especially pp. 46-47, 51, 61, 71. A fuller transcript is at the Catholic Archives of Texas, Austin. Also at the Catholic Archives is a photocopy of John Timon's letter of February 14, 1841, to an unknown person, possibly Joseph Rosati, which reports lodging with Dubois de Saligny, but does not specify *where*. The original of this letter is in the Vincentian Archives, Cabinet 4, Shelf 3, Box 5, University of Notre Dame Archives. Nor does the other source cited by Bayard specify the east Austin location: Timon's *Barrens Memoir*, 45, in the Archives of St. Mary's Seminary, Perryville, Missouri.

[13]See note 9 above, and George S. McIntosh to Guizot, July 4, 1841, in Garrison, *Diplomatic Correspondence*, III, 1345–1346.

[14]Dubois to Thiers, November 6, 1840, in Barker, *French Legation*, I, 170-171.

[15]On Pluyette and Baudin, see note 5 above. Baudin's advertisement appeared in the Austin *City Gazette*, November 24, 1841.

[16]Isaac Van Zandt to Mrs. Isaac Van Zandt, December 6, 1840, quoted in Stanley Siegel, *A Political History of the Texas Republic, 1836–45* (Austin: 1956; New York: 1973), p. 159. A photocopy of the original letter is in the Isaac Van Zandt Papers, Barker Texas History Center, University of Texas at Austin.

[17]For a good summary of the Franco-Texian bill, see Barker, *French Legation*, I, 193n.

[18]On the connection between Dulong's store and the Santa Fe trade, see the *Texas Sentinel*, October 24, 1840.

[19]Dubois to Thiers, June 26, 1840, in Barker, *French Legation*, I, 153.

[20]Dubois to Mayfield, March 21, 1841, in ibid., I, 229.

[21]Bullock to Burnet, February 20, 1841, in ibid., I, 213-214.

[22]The remarkably graphic testimony of Moses Johnson and Jules Dulong is preserved in Garrison, *Diplomatic Correspondence*, III, 1334.

[23]Dubois to Mayfield, February 19, 1841, in ibid., III, 1289.

[24]Dubois to Mayfield, February 24, 1841, in ibid., III, 1298.

[25]Dubois to Guizot, March 1, 1841, in Barker, *French Legation*, I, 211–212, and Mayfield to Dubois, March 21, 1841, in Garrison, *Diplomatic Correspondence*, III, 1312.

[26]Dubois to Guizot, March 1, 1841, in Barker, *French Legation*, I, 210.

²⁷Dubois to Mayfield, March 25, 1841, in ibid., I, 230–231.

²⁸Ibid., I, 231; Mayfield was quoted in Dubois to Guizot, February 16, 1841, in ibid., I, 202.

²⁹Quoted in Siegel, *Political History*, 161.

³⁰Mr. Cosmao to Ministry of the Navy and Colonies, May 16, 1841, in Barker, *French Legation*, I, 240, and a series of letters from Dubois to Guizot: February 10, 1842, ibid., 283–286; February 26, 1842, ibid., 289–291; March 16, 1842, ibid., 293–295; April 18, 1842, ibid., 307; and June 29, 1842, ibid., 341-342. All these were sent from New Orleans, except the last, which was sent from Galveston.

³¹Barker, *French Legation*, II, *passim*; Guizot's comment was written on Dubois to Guizot, April 18, 1845, in Barker, *French Legation*, II, 652.

³²Ashbel Smith, *Reminiscences of the Texas Republic* (Galveston: 1876), 32, 34; Barker, *French Legation*, I, 23.

³³Barker, *French Legation*, I, 24-32.

³⁴Ibid., I, 32–33.

³⁵Ibid., I, 170–71.

³⁶Deed Book, Travis County Courthouse, Austin, vol. Q, 561–564; "beautiful piece of property" in Dubois to Guizot, November 6, 1840, in Barker, *French Legation*, I, 170.

³⁷Barker, *French Legation*, I, 170–171; see also note 11 above.

³⁸Deed Book, Travis County Courthouse, vol. Q, 561–564.

³⁹*Texas Democrat* (Austin), August 16, 1848, and August 30, 1848. On the protection of the view to the Capitol, see the Austin *American Statesman*, February 15, 1985, B1.

⁴⁰On Thomas William Ward, see his obituary in the *Daily Democratic Statesman* (Austin), November 20, 1872; on his schooling with the East India Company, see H. M. Vibart, *Addiscombe: Its Heroes and Men of Note* (Westminster: 1894), p. 668; on the Capitol at Houston, see the contract between Ward and Augustus Chapman Allen, February 18, 1837, in the Acts of William Christy, 377–380, Notarial Archives of New Orleans.

⁴¹That Ward owned some of Dubois's furniture is attested by Virginia Wilson Spence to Emma Kyle Burleson, June 21, 1907, in the French Embassy Collection, 2-23/1051, Texas State Archives, Austin.

⁴²Advertisements for these sawmills may be found in the Austin *City Gazette*, July 29, 1840, and the *Texas Sentinel*, October 24, 1840.

⁴³Austin *City Gazette*, February 3, 1841; on ram's head hinges, see Samuel Wilson, Jr., Roulhac Toledano, Sally Kittredge Evans, and Mary Louise Christovich, *New Orleans Architecture: The Creole Fauburgs* (Gretna: 1974), 48–49.

⁴⁴Asher Benjamin, *The American Builder's Companion* (Boston: 1806; 6th ed., 1827; reprint New York: 1969), 34.

⁴⁵Daughters of the Republic of Texas, *Legation de France a la Republique de Texas* (Austin: 1970), 5.

⁴⁶Dorris L. Olds, *The French Legation Kitchen* (Austin: 1967), which is the report of the Texas Archeological Research Laboratory, University of Texas at Austin.

[47]Ibid.

[48]See note 11 above.

[49]*Texas Sentinel*, August 19, 1841.

[50]Anson Jones to Mrs. Anson Jones, quoted in Herbert Gambrell, *Anson Jones: The Last President of Texas* (New York: 1948), 220.

[51]Julia Nott Waugh, *Castro-ville and Henry Castro: Empresario* (San Antonio: 1934), 2; Barker, *French Legation*, I, 300–303.

[52]Henry Jewett, "The Archives War of Texas," *DeBow's Review*, I, no. 5 (May 1859), 517–518. Jewett, an early Austin settler, wrote that Dubois de Saligny raised the flag over his home, but Dubois's own correspondence places him in New Orleans at the time (see note 30 above). Seventeen years had blurred Jewett's memory, for it would have been the servants who took the liberty of raising the French flag.

[53]Odin in Kirwin, *Diamond Jubilee*, 77; W. Eugene Hollan and R. L. Butler, *William Bollaert's Texas* (Norman: 1956), 195.

[54]Mary Starr Barkley, *History of Travis County and Austin* (Waco: 1963), 156; *Texas Democrat* (Austin), August 16, 1848, and August 30, 1848.

[55]Lois Douglas, *Dr. Joseph William Robertson, 1809–1870* (Austin: 1981), copies at the Austin History Center of the Austin Public Library, and at the French Legation Museum; and James M. Coleman, *Aesculapius on the Colorado: The Story of Medical Practice in Travis County to 1899* (Austin: 1971), 9, 12, 15–17.

[56]Douglas, *Joseph William Robertson*. Julia Lee Sinks, the sister of Lydia Lee Robertson, wrote a series of articles on life in early Austin, which appeared in the Galveston *News* and the Dallas *News* in January and February of 1896. The Austin History Center has transcripts of some of these articles.

[57]Douglas, *Joseph William Robertson*.

[58]The lattice on the porch is visible in numerous late nineteenth and early twentieth century views of the house. On the additional room attached to the kitchen and on Maria the cook, see Irma Robertson to Mrs. Maurice Plumb, September 27, 1961, a copy of which is in the records of the Texas Archeological Research Laboratory, University of Texas at Austin. Irma Robertson was a granddaughter of Joseph and Lydia Robertson.

[59]The date of the fire is uncertain. The original kitchen is visible in the Augustus Koch aerial view of Austin done in 1873, and the new attached kitchen is visible in another aerial view of 1893. Robertson family tradition assigns a date ca. 1880. The Robertson wing was demolished ca. 1954. The only record of its appearance is a single photograph of the exterior made in 1934 by Louis C. Page, Jr.; the original is in the Library of Congress, Washington, D.C., and a copy is in the Austin History Center.

[60]On Lillie Robertson, see *Fifty Years of Achievement: History of the Daughters of the Republic of Texas* (Dallas: 1942), 156, 158, and 162.

[61]On Louis C. Page, Jr., see *Austin: Its Architects and Architecture (1836–1986)* (Austin: 1986), 74. The Historic American Buildings Survey drawings of the Legation are in the Library of Congress; a set of tracings are in the Austin Archi-

tectural Archives at the Austin History Center.

[62]On the DRT, see *Fifty Years of Achievement, and Ninety Years of the Daughters: History of the Daughters of the Republic of Texas* (Waco: 1981).

[63]The most important resource on the restoration of the house is the series of *Proceedings of the Annual Convention of the Daughters of the Republic of Texas*. On the efforts of the state to purchase the Legation, see the *1945 Annual*, 43–47, 69; the *1946 Annual*, 83; and the *1947 Annual*, 58–60, 111–113.

[64]*1950 Annual*, 35-36, 49, 91–92, 95; *1951 Annual*, 118–119.

[65]*1952 Annual*, 100–101; the Stautz-Mabry plan is illustrated in a brochure, *Légation de France*, on file at the French Legation Museum; *1955 Annual*, 73–74.

[66]*1953 Annual*, 132–133; interview with Mr. C. Coatsworth Pinkney, November 19, 1986.

[67]One of A. Watt Harris's specification drawings is in the Austin Architectural Archives at the Austin History Center; A. W. Harris to Edna Hinde, June 27, 1953, and February 21, 1955, and Edna Hinde to A. W. Harris, January 28, 1955, in the files of the French Legation Museum.

[68]*1955 Annual*, 73.

[69]Rudolph Hendric to Mrs. Frank Davol, November 10, 1954, and "Report of the French Legation Restoration Committee," November 12, 1954, both in the files of the French Legation Museum.

[70]*1956 Annual*, 41–49; *1957 Annual*, 60–62; Mrs. Margaret Barclay Megarity to DRT members, November 15, 1955, in the files of the French Legation Museum; and *Légation de France a la République de Texas*. On Stripling, see Michael McCullar, *Restoring Texas: Raiford Stripling's Life and Architecture* (College Station: 1985), especially 129–133.

[71]Megarity to DRT members, November 15, 1955.

[72]*1956 Annual*, 41–47; *Légation de France a la République de Texas*.

[73]Olds, *The French Legation Kitchen*; McCullar, *Restoring Texas*, 133; a set of photocopies of Stripling's plans for the kitchen are in the files of the French Legation Museum.

[74]*1974 Annual*, 89; *1975 Annual*, 101; and McCullar, *Restoring Texas*, 133.

[75]Interviews with Mrs. Lois Douglas, March 1987.

[76]This section is heavily indebted to Joan Clay Lowe's thorough evaluation of all artifacts in the Legation, which is on file at the French Legation Museum. On Dubois's furniture, see Virginia Wilson Spence to Emma Kyle Burleson, June 21, 1907, in the French Embassy Collection, 2–23/1051, Texas State Archives, Austin.

[77]On Hannig, see Lonn Taylor and David B. Warren, *Texas Furniture* (Austin: 1975), 295-296.

About the Author

Kenneth Hafertepe is a cultural historian specializing in American art and architectural history. He has earned a bachelor's degree in government from Georgetown University in Washington, D.C., and a Ph.D. in American civilization from the University of Texas at Austin. He is the author of *America's Castle: The Evolution of the Smithsonian Building and Its Institution, 1840–1878,* and one of the principal essays in *Austin: Its Architects and Architecture,* recently published by the Austin Chapter of the American Institute of Architects and the Heritage Society of Austin. He has also written articles and book reviews for journals such as *The Texas Humanist, Texas Architect, Design Book Review,* and the *Journal of the Society of Architectural Historians.* Dr. Hafertepe has taught in the American Studies Program at the University of Texas at Austin, and has spoken to numerous groups on topics related to American art and architecture.